IN THE
CROSSHAIRS

IN THE CROSSHAIRS

God's Urgent Message
to America
in the 2017/2024
Solar Eclipses

James F. Fitzgerald

IN THE CROSSHAIRS

Published by Watchword Worldwide
Ambridge, PA 15003

TheEndTimeExpert.com

Published 2024
First Edition 2024
Printed in the United States of America

ISBN 978-1-57466-205-4 pbk
ISBN 978-1-57466-206-1 ebook
ISBN 978-1-57466-207-8 audiobook

Contents

PART ONE

The 2017/2024 Solar Eclipses: Discerning Their Meaning

Many wonder what, if anything, the second total solar eclipse could mean this April 8th—being one of two in seven years that will create a great "X" over the heart of the United States. The first in August 2017, earned the title, The Great American Eclipse, with its path confined to the U.S. alone, an exceedingly rare event.

Since then, numerous commentators have offered various opinions about what the two American eclipses could signify. Without question, some have provided truly incredible details and insights after years of research. We owe them a debt of gratitude. Many think the two solar signs could portend troubling times ahead for our country.

Nevertheless, the meaning of these crossing eclipses isn't about speculations or opinions. Scripture tells us, "If the trumpet gives an uncertain sound, who will get ready for battle?" (1 Cor. 14:8). We should believe, then, that the Lord is not giving us an uncertain message through these two unique eclipses. As we will see, his alarm is extremely clear, every bit as clear as Jonah's warning to Nineveh. Only in America's case there will be no great repentance as happened with Nineveh, telling us that God's judgment is determined and sure. It's also astonishingly prophetic.

I. Interpreting the Signs by Prophecy

To discern God's message in the crossing solar signs correctly, however, requires three essential keys: belief in heavenly signs, an accurate eschatology, and a right understanding of the physical signs themselves. The problem is Christians and commentators fail to understand the meaning of the combined eclipses for these three reasons.

First, most believers fail to understand them due to their basic skepticism about the existence of divine signs in the heavens at all or not taking them seriously. At their heart, such thinking results from biblical ignorance, spiritual unbelief, or complacency and disinterest. But none of these attitudes has a place in the Christian life. They rather call for repentance and faith.

Second, even for those who believe in the significance of these solar signs, they fail to see or know their true end-time context. Many may think they do. Many even have practical insights. But still, without an accurate prophetic perspective, they miss the heart of the matter. And this leads to not rightly applying God's word to interpreting the signs for their real meaning. So, they remain uncommitted, or flounder here and there, guessing or grasping at straws.

And third, even for those who observe the amazing details in the two eclipses, they simply misinterpret the providential meaning of the eclipses that form an "X" over America. As we'll see in Part Two, this comes from Christians not understanding the real nature of the things to which the eclipses so clearly point. And the reasons for this are both theological and historical.

However, by the end of this message, you yourself will know with certainty the meaning of the two remarkable heavenly signs occurring over the U.S. in 2017 and 2024.

A. Biblical Grounds for Signs in the Sky

To address the reason of unbelief, we must first examine Genesis 1:14, where God reveals the four reasons for creating the sun, moon, and stars. The later three are for telling time, but the Lord's primary reason is for "signs." So, the Creator himself tells us that his principal purpose for placing these bright objects in the sky was to give signs. Who are we, then, to doubt God's word, or to question him who gave it?

Further, King David wrote in Psalm 19, that the Lord speaks through the heavens in a language that everyone on earth can understand. The psalmist says: "Day unto day utters speech, and night unto night shows knowledge. There is no speech nor language, where their voice is not heard" (Ps. 19:2-3). Therefore, we can believe that God will speak through these extraordinary and unique solar eclipses and do so in a language we can comprehend.

Working together in this way, Scripture and providence will then guide our discernment so we can know the sure meaning of these special solar events. Yet though even unbelievers can tell time, signs require faith. But be prepared to be shocked. The Church is so generally out of touch with where we are prophetically that the truth will be sobering and hard for many to take.

B. Prophetic Context for the Eclipses

The second and chief reason for misinterpreting the meaning of the two solar eclipses comes down to a simple fact: Christian leaders, teachers, and believers don't know, understand, or believe where we are in relation to end-time prophecy. And, while many may think they do, their statements and opinions reveal they don't. Being committed to unbiblical views, their minds are then closed already to seeing or hearing the truth, making them unable to interpret Scripture accurately. This also means they can't properly evaluate the eclipses in their prophetic context.

Most Christian leaders, however, pay little attention, making glib, lazy comments like the obligatory, "no one know the day or hour," or that it's pointless to try until the Lord shows up. Worse, they think this way though Jesus said to "watch" and "when you see these things, look up, for your redemption draws nigh." But denying the Lord's plain instructions, they persist in their disobedience and woeful unbelief. Instead of preaching the word, they only parrot what they've heard, being misled and misleading others.

Sadly, despite the countless hours of teaching on YouTube, the endless books, and those few pulpits that do deal with it, there may not be a hundred Christians in America who can accurately identify precisely where we are in God's end-time program. For unlike the noble Bereans, who didn't just take Paul's word for things but did their own biblical verification, preachers and teachers typically pass on only what they've heard in matters of eschatology.

Yet, in relation to the two eclipses, once we do understand where we are in God's prophetic plan, as you will see, the meaning of the solar signs will be crystal clear, painfully so.

1) Fulfillment of End-Time Prophecy

Of first importance, then, believers must know that the sign of the crossing solar eclipses delivers a distinct end-time message to America. Their prophetic context is what reveals this to be true. More particularly, targeting the United States as they do with an "X," they foretell the imminent fulfillment of a specific end-time prophecy about to strike the U.S., to then be followed by three subsequent prophecies over three short years. The Church and commentators miss all this entirely. It's a big deal with profound implications for America, Israel, and the world.

Specifically, the intersection of the two eclipses heralds the approach of *the second birth pang* that Jesus foretold in Matthew 24. In chronological order, this sign is number two of the five initial end-time signs that Jesus outlined in verses six through eight. The first has occurred, the second is at hand, and the last three will follow shortly after.

About the second birth pang, the Lord said, "For nation shall rise against nation and kingdom against kingdom" (Matt. 24:7a). But upon hearing this, most believers will dismiss it outright. They will say this sign is far too vague to serve as a definitive guide for the end times. They will shrug that things like this have always happened ever since the time of Christ. Nations and kingdoms have always fought each other. How, then, could such a general prophecy guide us now? It doesn't reveal anything new or specific. There is no possible way for us to know what this sign means exactly and certainly not until after the eclipse happens and events occur.

2) Prophetic Ignorance and Unbelief

But such thinking about the prophetic birth pangs is entirely wrong. Believers fail to understand that Jesus later recast the first four labor pains in another form that was far more detailed. Six decades after his Olivet Discourse, he sent his angel to John with the book of Revelation and its seven closed seals.

Popular culture even knows the first four seals as the fabulous Four Horsemen of the Apocalypse. But the fact is these famed Four Horsemen are none other than Jesus' first four birth pangs. They are the very same things. They are the same in nature, number, and order. And the first four seals are packed with additional information to guide our discernment.

But again, because Christians by and large misinterpret the Four Horsemen, as well as their timing, they are prevented from discerning these events when they occur. And this is most unfortunate because the Four Horsemen of Revelation give us a great deal of insight in a concise space due to the use of symbolism. This is particularly true regarding the first and second horsemen who parallel the first and second birth pangs. And if the eclipses herald the second birth pang, they warn of the coming of the second horseman of the Apocalypse, too.

3) Interpretation and Timing

The trouble with symbols, however, is people can make them mean whatever they want. But the key to correctly interpreting the symbols in Revelation is seeing them through the Lord's Olivet teaching, where he described the first four birth pangs in plain language. And in doing so, we apply the principle that Scripture interprets Scripture. What is clear also helps interpret the less clear.

And so it is in this case. Jesus' Olivet Discourse is the key to accurately interpreting the symbolism in Revelation. It's impossible to do otherwise.

Moreover, the issue of timing is equally important. Jesus taught that the initial birth pangs would begin a final generation lasting almost forty years (Matt. 24:34). And it would begin with the first birth pang: "You'll hear of wars and rumors of wars."

And while Christians may react again to the vagueness of this sign, when paired with the first of the seven seals, it becomes tremendously enlightening. That's because the first birth pang refers to the first of the Four Horsemen, the rider on the white horse who goes off "conquering and to conquer." And his historical ride then starts the end times that last almost forty years, not seven as so many mistakenly teach, causing enormous confusion and harm. That's why it is critical for us to establish the prophetic context regarding the sign of the American solar eclipses.

4) Misidentifying the White-Horse Rider

Nevertheless, the related problem becomes the ridiculous and nonsensical belief endlessly propounded that the first of the Four Horsemen is Antichrist who makes a deceitful treaty with the Jews. But if this first rider comes at the start of the end-time generation that lasts almost 40 years, how can he be Antichrist? He doesn't appear until at least the final seven. So, this interpretation is absurd on its face.

And equally foolish, this first rider can't be Jesus, as the reformers and many others have believed. The corresponding birth pang is *wars and rumors of wars*. And Jesus would hardly describe his work of proclaiming the Gospel for 2000 years as "wars and rumors of wars." So again, this interpretation is impossible.

Yet this process is precisely how the two different witnesses, Olivet and Revelation, work in tandem, hand in hand together, to guide our discernment and protect us from misinterpreting. Two witnesses also provide a fuller, more complete picture. And as Scripture teaches, a matter is established by the testimony of two witnesses (Matt. 18:16-19; Cor.

13:1). The book of Revelation doesn't stand alone. We have Jesus' complimentary testimony from Olivet. And so, the period of the seven seals covers almost forty years, a fact we could never know without the guidance of the Lord's Olivet Discourse. And this time starts with the rider on the white horse.

II. Where Are We Prophetically?

Now, then, if Jesus or Antichrist isn't the first rider of the Apocalypse who begins the end times, who is? Who should we be looking for as the critical white-horse rider? What other human could he be?

In reality, the rider on the white horse—the first of the Four Horsemen of the Apocalypse—has been riding before our eyes since after 9/11. But due to the Church's faulty eschatology and unbelief, it's been blind to this fact for twenty-three years.

A. Identifying the White-Horse Rider

Exactly *seven days* after the attack, sitting in *the White House*, the president of the United States of America, the leader of the most powerful nation in world history, signed into law the War on Terror on September 18, 2001, which was also *the Feast of Trumpets*. And like the first of a pair of prophetic bookends, it pointed to Christ's future return in victory during that same feast with the sound of a cosmic trumpet in the heavens. In its significance, the signing of this law by our president echoed the biblical decrees and edicts of Cyrus, Darius, and Artaxerxes.

But this isn't the time or the place to defend or prove these things. I've written three books in great detail about them, the first being, *The 9/11 Prophecy*, originally released as an e-book in 2007 and republished as a hardback in 2013, briefly becoming the #1 Religious Essay on Amazon. The second is a novel, The End-Time Expert, published in paperback this past December 2023. And the third presents an overview of the end times in a nutshell, Your

Biblical Guide to the End of the World, to be released on Amazon in the summer of 2024.

B. The Beginning of the Endtimes

Tragically, due to its abject lack of understanding and general ignorance in eschatology, an oblivious Church still doesn't recognize the start of the end-time generation. But the end times started on 9/11. The Lord's final generation began in New York City at precisely 8:46 AM on that day and hour. And this was confirmed seven days later by the rider on the white horse going out, "conquering and to conquer," or as Jesus called it, "wars and rumors of wars."

But since the Church didn't perceive the first of the Four Horsemen, it's also not in a place to recognize the coming of the second horseman, the rider on the red horse. And this is crucial because this second rider will end the riding of the white horse: the United States, which is the location of the total solar eclipses.

Furthermore, John tells us that the rider on the red horse "will remove all peace from the earth by means of a great sword" (Rev. 6:3-4).

In our day, such a sword could only mean a WMD, a weapon of mass destruction that will initiate all-out nuclear war. Again, Jesus described this time as the second birth pang, when "nation will rise against nation and kingdom against kingdom."

Without the guidance of an accurate eschatology for context and content, however, we could only speculate about the meaning of the 2017/2024 eclipses. But because of the end-time prophecies of Jesus and John, we can be assured of their meaning: these two prophetic eclipses announce the imminent outpouring of God's wrath that will begin with a nuclear WWIII that targets America—the white horse and its rider.

C. Identifying the Red-Horse Rider

Now, analyzing today's world in light of John's prophecy, we can see five nuclear powers on one hand, and perhaps five or six opposing nuclear powers on the other. The red-horse prophecy further implies that this rider will act preemptively to start the nuclear world war that removes all peace from the Earth. Of necessity, this will include Israel and the near certain destruction of Tel Aviv, its capital before its relocation to Jerusalem in 2017—the year of the Great American Eclipse.

And of all the planet's nuclear powers, Russia, fighting in Ukraine, has the world's largest nuclear arsenal, which it continues to develop, as well as its hypersonic missile delivery systems. On recent multiple occasions, Russian leaders have also threatened the preemptive use of these weapons against the United States and England if pushed.

And lastly, in the former USSR, Russia founded the world's first *Red Communist* nation, which also mobilized the huge victorious *Red Army* in the last world war. Russia's Putin is even on record saying that his country's greatest disaster was the breakup of the USSR. Russia is also aligned with our nuclear enemy, *Red China*, as well as in alliance with the world's foremost state-sponsor of terrorism, fanatical Iran, actively developing its own nuclear weapons.

D. The Coming Nuclear WWIII

This prophetic nuclear war is now imminent. The rapture isn't as many believe and teach—some wishfully linking it to the April eclipse. WWIII is imminent. And though many do foresee this danger with Russia, China, or Iran, they fail to understand that it will fulfill John's Revelation 6:3-4 prophecy, and what that then reveals about the future. For the solar signs also point us to the remaining horsemen, not only the second rider. Even the seven-year period directs us to Revelation, with its seven seals, where that number appears no less than fifty-five times.

Prophetically, then, this is the end-time context and meaning of the America-specific total solar eclipses that will mark our nation for judgment with a perfect X on April 8. Poised like a dagger at the heart of the first horseman of the Apocalypse, this eclipse warns of the red-horse rider bringing imminent nuclear world war, *and by extension,* the third and fourth horsemen who will follow with their consequences of global famine and pestilence to ravage the Earth.

Yet even then that's not all there is to come. On Olivet, Jesus also outlined a fifth initial birth pang. In Revelation, this is the sixth seal with its terrible double judgment. As we'll see in Part Two, the crossing solar eclipses indicate that it will also hit the U.S. And with that, God's particular wrath against America will end for the time being.

But incredibly, for those who say the United States is not to found in Revelation or in the end times, they couldn't be more wrong. All five of Jesus' initial birth pangs will target our nation in particular; hence the sign of the solar X. America is the first white horse in Revelation, too. It's also Paul's last restrainer of the lawless one that must be removed. And the Lord's initial birth pangs will help remove it from power to prepare the way for Antichrist.

So, having much more to say, we will embellish on all these in Part Two, including their shocking timing and outcome, as we go further to discern the meaning of the awesome patterns and providential signs in the eclipses themselves. They deal with the Civil War and more—but are all being widely misunderstood, as well.

Nevertheless, as America experiences judgment, Christians must remember that Jesus referred to these painful events as "birth pangs" for a reason and told us not to be alarmed or troubled. We're to look beyond earthly suffering to the birth of a kingdom that will never end. It draws ever closer with the Lord's return at the end of this generation that began on 9/11.

PART TWO

PART TWO

Remarkable Signs in the Two Eclipses

Now to discern the meaning in the signs of the two total solar eclipses themselves. As numerous authors, teachers, and commentators have shown, the 2017/2024 eclipses reveal extraordinary patterns in their crisscrossing of the U.S. These signs deal with the Civil War, Salem, Nineveh, Jonah, Lincoln, Jesus, Satan, and more. Yet, as Christians have missed the prophetic end-time context of the two eclipses, they also fail to see the clear meaning conveyed in their providential signs—due to misunderstanding the real historical and spiritual natures of the things to which they point. While the Church should excel in discernment, it fails miserably.

But, as we saw in Part One, we do understand their end-time context; and now, as you will see, much of the true meaning of the solar signs, too. Yet, even then, the key remains knowing their prophetic context. Without knowing that, we could only speculate about

God's purpose in the signs, even if we did understand their meaning.

I. The Civil War Signs

On August 21, 2017, having started in our northwest, the first total eclipse ended in our southeast over Fort Sumter, where the Civil War began in 1861. Remarkably, the solar eclipse on April 8 ended in our northeast and began in our southwest over Eagle Pass, Texas, where the very last action in the Civil War occurred. That happened when Confederate General Shelby refused to surrender and crossed the Rio Grande into Mexico on Independence Day, July 4, 1865, months after Appomattox.

So, with incredible specificity, the 2024 solar eclipse started where the Civil War ended, and the 2017 eclipse ended where the Civil War began—the bloodiest war the U.S. ever fought. During that four-year conflict, one of every ten men of fighting age in the country died from wounds, disease, or starvation. In fact, it literally "decimated" America's male population of military age, killing one in ten, as the original word meant from the Roman *deci*, for ten.

And due to their obvious connection with our Civil War, some think the eclipses may point to an impending civil war or issues like state's rights, where Texas seeks to protect its border from illegal immigration at Eagle Pass, while the federal government opposes them.

But such views about our Civil War—seeing it from a purely secular perspective—miss the point entirely. To accurately interpret the Civil War signs, we must understand the conflict's true meaning. And for that purpose, we can do no better than to hear Abraham Lincoln's mature view. The sign of the 2017 eclipse even tells us so. The first eclipse began over *Lincoln City*, Oregon. And more than merely one more Civil War connection, this sign directs us. We're meant to see the signs that follow from the war president's deeply informed and spiritual perspective.

A. God's Purpose in Our Civil War

In his second inaugural address, Lincoln told his hearers that the conflict served as God's judgment on our country for its sin of slavery and the war wouldn't end until it satisfied justice. In poetic terms, he said that demanded "a swipe of the sword for every crack of the whip."

Today, historians estimate that slavers stole 620,000 men, women, and children from Africa and imported them into North America during the era of slavery. Ironically, some 620,000 people then died in the Civil War from battle and disease. It made for a one-to-one ratio.

I wrote about these things extensively in my three books. The war demonstrated that God, who hates injustice, kept his promise that "vengeance is mine and I will repay." Furthermore, in his divine holiness and righteousness, he punishes corporate sin with corporate judgment. And our Civil War remains the Lord's greatest judgment on our nation for its sin, a sin from which it repented, officially ending chattel slavery in 1863 after Lincoln's Emancipation Proclamation.

And for those who would still question a spiritual view of our Civil War, consider the striking providence that Lee surrendered at Appomattox on Palm Sunday and Lincoln was assassinated in that Holy Week on Good Friday.

B. God's Wrath for Sin

But how does God's purpose in the Civil War relate to the two solar eclipses targeting America? Why would he send a message about that now through these solar signs? Because of our current sin, the Lord wants us to remember his last great judgment on a grievous national sin.

And what would our sin be now?

Before he died, Dr. R.C. Sproul, perhaps the country's leading theologian, said ten years ago that he believed abortion was worse than the diabolical institution of slavery. If correct, consider what that means in light of the Civil War's one-to-one ratio. If God took the lives of 620,000 Americans over the sin of stealing

620,000 slaves from Africa, what will he do to a nation that has now murdered over 65,000,000 babies in the womb?

The fact is the Lord has forbidden the unwarranted killing of innocent people in his sixth commandment: "Thou shalt do no murder." That being the case, what will a holy God do in justice to an insolent nation that legalized the killing of at least 65 million unborn babies over a period of more than fifty years? The Civil War gives us the precedent. And the solar eclipses deliver the warning.

Further, for those who would argue abortion remains a matter between a woman and her doctor, they overlook the corporate nature of their sin that demands a corporate punishment. The whole country will suffer for it, as happened over slavery. Moreover, pointing unmistakably to the Civil War as they do, the solar signs confirm the coming of imminent war to America. They further call us to see its moral justification and to prepare for the dreadful outcome of God's judgments. And its prophetic context points to an apocalyptic WWIII and its results.

C. The Outcome of God's Judgments

And here again, an accurate eschatology can aid us to correctly interpret the signs in the two eclipses. Having established their end-time context, specifically during the riding of the white horse, we can believe they foretell the coming of the red-horse rider who will initiate a preemptive nuclear war with the United States, fulfilling Matthew 24:7 and Revelation 6:3-4. Even now, we see providence putting the pieces in place through Putin's war with Ukraine and the Hamas attack on Israel. And again, as terrible as a nuclear WWIII scenario already appears, John says *the third and fourth horsemen* will follow on its heels with famine and pestilence.

And beyond that, the apostle foretells their awful outcome in summarizing the results. As John writes in his inspired vision, the three combined horsemen will kill a quarter of all the people living on earth. With a global population approaching 8 billion, a quarter of that number means almost two billion human beings will die in the remaining Four Horsemen judgments.

Then applying that same horrifying percentage to the U.S. population, upwards of 85 million people or more could die in America by nuclear war, famine, and pestilence. And they will include Christians and non-Christians, as both died alike in the Civil War. Not surprisingly, when contemplating the extent of our national sin, considering the number of abortions, that sobering number falls within the realm of expectation, commensurate with what divine justice would lead us to expect as punishment. Only God knows the true accounting.

D. The Timing of WWIII

In terms of this coming war's timing, prophecy and providence may indicate when— even to the day and hour. Again, Jesus called his end-time signs, "birth pangs." While the final generation lasts nearly 40 years, birth pangs come at the end of a birth process lasting *forty-weeks*, or more popularly known as nine months. Could this timing apply to the start of WWIII?

We have precedence. Going back nine months before 9/11 and the beginning of the end times, we discover a striking phenomenon. It involves the contested election of President George W. Bush, who became the first white-horse rider. His election required a rare and controversial decision by the Supreme Court to confirm him as president. That happened on December 12th, 2000, *nine months* to the day to September 11, 2001, that started the first "birth pang" and called out the first horseman. Too significant for coincidence, this exact timing seems a confirmation.

If we then apply the same forty-week/nine-month period to after the eclipse on April 8, it takes us to January 2025. Incredibly, that's when America inaugurates its next president in Washington, D.C., which also suffered attack at the start of the end times, a harbinger of sorts. A most special event, the inauguration of our president happens only once every four to eight years.

If the red-horse rider then launched its preemptive nuclear attack on the United States *at noon on January 20*, it couldn't pick a more strategic opportunity. Our government heads will fill the nation's capital. Potentially, the complete leadership of two different administrations will attend, not just one, including two presidents, two vice-presidents, two cabinets; all of Congress, the Supreme Court, the heads of all Federal branches, and the nation's top military brass, all assembled in one place at one time.

Regardless of the actual date, however, strategy will make Washington, D.C. a primary target in WWIII. To launch a nuclear attack on the U.S. without first cutting off its head would be folly. And Russia's leaders have warned they will take out Washington and London if pushed.

In a form of poetic justice, then, the red horse would finish off the white horse where it began its prophetic ride over two decades earlier. What could make more sense of these things? And if any should yet question the divine justification, this Easter Sunday the week before the April 8 eclipse, the nation's chief executive, speaking in that capacity—and in his office as the white-horse-rider—boldly proclaimed the day that celebrates the glorious resurrection of the Son of God to be one of gross sexual perversion. The president's offense filled up the full measure of America's wickedness. And causing the deaths of tens of millions in early 2025, WWIII will set the stage for famine and pestilence, the third and fourth birth pangs to kill tens of millions more.

II. The Fifth "Birth Pang"

Yet even then God's terrible judgment on our country remains unfinished. Further signs in the eclipses point to additional end-time prophecies. Beyond the other connections to the Civil War, the crossing eclipses meet right upon the Mason-Dixon Line that separated north and south during the time of slavery. Remarkable in itself, their X falls not just anywhere on the old line of separation, however, but where the Mississippi and Ohio Rivers meet, drawing our attention to the joining of the vast watershed from the West with that from the East. In many ways, this providential X truly marks the center of the United States of America.

But this awful specificity may indicate much more. It may even point to the locations of the coming birth pangs, from first to last.

A. Pittsburgh: the Source of the Ohio

The Ohio River starts in Pittsburgh. But before 9/11, so that the fountainhead of the Ohio might become famous for God, the Lord chose Pittsburgh for the source of his warning about an imminent, prophetic, surprise attack that would start the end times. On 9/11, the final generation began with Jesus' first "birth pang" and the opening of John's first seal, all confirmed then by the subsequent riding of the white horse. Again, I tell in my books how God used our production of *The Book of Revelation* for his deliberate warning. And with that understanding, we released the first ever word-for-word production of the Bible's most prophetic book in the Millennium year at Madison Square Garden in July 2000. It then premiered in the heart of New York City 430 days before the attack—reflecting the exact number of days of Ezekiel's warning before Jerusalem's destruction by Babylon. Yet who believed it?

Moreover, when the Lord sent us from Pittsburgh to knowingly warn New York through *The Book of Revelation*, I'd immediately thought of Jonah and Nineveh, but reasoned that God must have predetermined his judgment on the city because its people wouldn't know or repent to avert it. Fourteen months later 9/11 struck with devastating results.

Now, as I write this message about the solar signs, it seems so much like it did twenty-four years ago when the Lord spoke to me through his word and providence and sent us with his warning before 9/11. The Scripture even says, "Then the word of the Lord came to Jonah *a second time*" (Jon. 3:1)! Only now the Lord has conveyed his message through two American eclipses with clear connections to Revelation, even to Jesus' name in the sky. The placement of the solar X may even signify that prophetic Pittsburgh itself could die bearing testimony to the "second birth pang" and to the red-horse rider's nuclear attack on the U. S. and its cities.

B. Yellowstone: the Mississippi Drainage

To the west, the Mississippi drains all the way to the Rocky Mountains where the Lord's fifth and final initial birth pang may strike. In foretelling the end-time birth pangs, Jesus placed earthquakes after pestilence. In Revelation's sixth seal judgment, a great earthquake like-wise follows the Four Horsemen. In its description and the Greek word used, however, this quake most likely speaks of a massive volcanic eruption, one that could explode where our planet's largest active volcano resides in the Rockies at Yellowstone Park. In fact, in its path of totality, the 2017 eclipse passed over Yellowstone's lower corner.

The vastness of this volcano's destructive power is almost incomprehensible. Mt. St. Helen's, by comparison, blew *forty cubic miles* of debris into the atmosphere. Yet Yellowstone would throw more than *600 cubic miles* of volcanic material into the air. Burning lava would also bury the local area for miles around. And ash and volcanic glass particles would blanket the rest of the country and circle the Earth on its jet stream, blackening the sun and turning the moon blood red. Their effects would carry on for years.

C. The Sixth Seal Asteroid

But even that catastrophe doesn't end the Lord's sixth seal judgment. Soon after the volcanic eruption, the largest asteroid to hit our planet in recorded history will make impact shortly before harvest time, quite possibly landing in America's breadbasket, also served by the Mississippi River system.

In his vision, John describes "stars" falling to earth like winter figs shaken from a tree (Rev. 6:12-17). With our advanced understanding of the heavens and our solar system today, however, we know that John couldn't have seen stars, but rather a large asteroid breaking up in our atmosphere, appearing as multiple falling stars. And with our modern cataloguing of more than 80% of large near-Earth Objects (NEOs), we also know that none of these space objects travel in packs near Earth. Moreover, they tell us that, while some large ones may pass relatively close, they project that none will hit us in the relative future.

Yet, since winter figs fall in August, John's prophetic description may be informative. Amazingly the closest of all the large NEO's known to pass us will do so in that same month shortly after the Four Horsemen. Asteroid 1999 AN10 will fly by our planet on August 7, 2027. Perhaps 9/10ths of a mile across, it will come within just 386,000 miles of Earth, zooming by at 26,000 mph. When astronomers first discovered it in 1999, this NEO terrified them, thinking it might strike us directly, but further calculations showed it wouldn't. Nevertheless, in the NEO index, they still categorize 1999 AN10 as a "Potentially Hazardous Asteroid." Quite possibly, therefore, the earlier supervolcano eruption might sufficiently alter Earth's gravitational forces to reel it in. Whatever happens, John's sixth seal prophecy assures us that an asteroid will impact the Earth in that timeframe and the only one known in that window remains 1999 AN10.

With this horrendous collision, the Lord Jesus will have completed his five initial birth pangs and six of the seven seals of Revelation. Beginning on 9/11, they include his judgments on America, the United States being the particular target of his wrath as signified by the X of the crossing eclipses yet having profound endtime repercussions for the whole world.

III. More Amazing Signs

Beyond what we've covered so far, we haven't even touched on a number of other startling signs in America's two solar eclipses. Without attempting to be exhaustive or addressing the rich signs in the starry Zodiac, we will examine six.

A. Seven Salem Cities

In its path of totality, the 2017 solar eclipse passed over or near seven U.S. cities named Salem. In fact, starting off, it crossed over Salem, Oregon, the first large city. And in a sign of further intentionality, some 40 miles north of the Mason Dixon line—at the exact spot where the 2017/2024 eclipses form their great X—sits a small farm road named Salem! The repetition of that name goes beyond coincidence.

Meaning *peace*, the word "Salem" has great biblical significance. For believers, nothing is more important than with peace with God, which we can only obtain by repentance and faith in Jesus Christ. In its Civil War context, the word "Salem" also reminds us that peace came to our nation only after its repentance from the sin of slavery. A unified Unites States then went on to become the superpower of the world and Paul's last restrainer. Biblically, then, the seven-fold repetition of Salem in the 2017 eclipse cries out for personal and national repentance as the only grounds for peace with God.

The word "Salem" also reminds us of Abraham's meeting with the mysterious ruler Melchizedek, an early type of Christ as we learn from Hebrews. Melchizedek ruled as King of Salem, meaning the King of Peace. And his city, the forerunner of Jerusalem, became the place where Christ died to purchase peace for sinners by paying for the sins of the world. In fact, the word Salem forms part of the name Jerusalem and turns our attention there.

Remarkably, Jerusalem became the Jewish capital in the year of the 2017 eclipse for the first time in 1947 years! It happened on December 6 and America played the key role. On that day, by presidential proclamation, the United States officially recognized Jerusalem as Israel's capital. The U.S. then moved its embassy there from Tel Aviv. And midway through the seven-year period between the two American eclipses, President Trump announced an unprecedented series of Middle East peace treaties named *The Abraham Accords*, brokered by America between Israel and its Muslim neighbors.

Finally, with its extraordinary sign of seven Salem cities, the 2017 solar eclipse calls Christians to fix their eyes on Jesus, *our peace* in the coming birth pangs. And returning at the end of this generation, the *Prince of Peace* will then establish his reign on Earth in the seventh millennium. For a thousand years, the lion and the lamb will lie down in peace together and men will sit quietly, "each under their vine and fig tree," a promise quoted throughout his lifetime by George Washington, the father and first president of the United States of America.

B. Seven Nineveh Cities

Incredibly, for the second of the six other signs, the 2024 eclipse will pass over or near another string of seven U.S. cities, these named Nineveh. Biblically important, too, it's where Jonah preached their doom within forty days. Assyria's ancient capital repented, however, averting destruction, a fact Jesus that himself acknowledged when he condemned the faithless Jews at his first coming. He said one greater than Jonah was in their midst, but they failed to recognize their Messiah, sealing their doom and the destruction of Jerusalem by the Romans.

Like the Jews, our people will also never repent en masse. They've gone too far too long to turn from their sins. And too complacent and fragmented to act in unity, the Church won't either for God to heal our land. By saying and hoping so, believers engage in wishful thinking.

The end times have begun and the U. S. must fall from a position of power to make way for Antichrist *in this generation*. Like a sign of Jonah, the seven times repetition of Nineveh—the number of completion—then testifies against America that her time is up with a forty-week warning. And it directs us to Revelation to discover God's coming judgments in the seven seals.

C. Alpha and Omega over the U.S.

In a third awesome sign, combining the 2017/2024 solar eclipses with the annular solar eclipse in October 2023 forms the first and last letters of the Hebrew alphabet above the United States. Amazingly, these two letters represent "alpha" and "omega" in the Greek, the very name that Jesus Christ assigned himself in Revelation. In verse 1:8, he said: "I am Alpha and Omega, the beginning and the end...." In effect, pointing to Revelation in the eclipses, Jesus signed his name over America.

Yet what does that mean? Considering its end-time context and everything else, we can assume significance. No doubt, we can see a kind of heavenly recognition honoring America's past role for good in a fallen world. In support of the Great Commission, it became the greatest sender, supporter, and protector of Christian missions in history. And the U.S. also became Paul's last restrainer of Antichrist.

But now in apostasy and disobedience, the United States finds itself under threat of imminent divine wrath. Ever since 9/11, it has only gotten worse in its moral abandonment and ungodliness. And like the writing on the wall for Babylon, or like a savor of death to those without the Gospel, the sign of Jesus' name written over America proclaims its approaching doom under apocalyptic judgment. The former city on a hill has become a place of darkness.

For believing Christians, however, Jesus' name in the heavens above reminds us of his promise that the end-time birth pangs will usher in his return when we join him in the sky. Indeed, he shouts from the heavens that our only hope lies in him. May God in his mercy and grace grant us a last Great Awakening to sweep many into his eternal kingdom!

D. Jesus Returns in This Generation

Now, reflecting on the two eclipses and the Second Coming, consider this special providence. Since Holy Week and Easter came early this year, they had to move the *Feast of the Annunciation of the Lord* past Easter to the day of the 2024 eclipse, April 8. And its assigned reading, Isaiah 7:12-14, proclaims *a sign* regarding the Lord's first coming. Isaiah's famous passage says, "Ask for a sign from the LORD, your God; let it be deep as the nether world, or high as the sky! Therefore, the Lord himself will give you this sign: the virgin shall be with child, and bear a son, and shall name him Emmanuel, which means "God is with us!"

What a wonderful sign to have this reading on April 8 that points to *a sign* of the Lord's first coming on the day of *the sign* pointing to his Second Coming. And that leads us to reflect even further on its timing in this specific generation.

When the Lord instructed his disciples on Mt. Olivet, he taught that the end times would last a little less than forty years. He said, "This generation shall not pass away before all these things take place." He also told them that after the tribulation of those days, "the sign of the Son of Man would appear in the heavens." And since the end times began in 2001, according to Jesus' authoritative teaching, this final generation can't extend past 2040. If we believe the Lord's words that means only 16 years now remain at most.

Then Paul wrote in 2 Thessalonians that the Lord won't return until two things happened first. One, an overall apostasy had to occur, a great falling away from the Christian faith where it once held sway. Of course, we find ourselves there today in America and in Western Civilization as a whole. Most now reject the historic Christian faith.

And Paul's second requirement stated that Antichrist must first appear—the lawless one whom the Lord will slay with the breath of his mouth at his coming. But Paul qualified that further by saying the lawless one won't appear until after that *which* and that *who* restrains him *is taken out of the way*. And while the restrainer's identity has long perplexed the Church, neither it, nor the Holy Spirit, nor angels qualify as the restrainer, as many foolishly believe today.

Instead, Paul taught in Romans that nations bear the sword to restrain evil. Historically, after the Empire embraced Christianity, Constantinople and the Eastern Empire restrained Islam's diabolical advance into Europe until all Europe became Christian, which then became the Lord's second restrainer and soundly defeated huge Islamic armies at Vienna in 1683. The United States, the world's current superpower, then became the third and last restrainer descended from a converted Roman Empire. But now the Lord must take the last restrainer out of the way for Antichrist to come in the last seven years of this generation. Eventually, he will rule over every nation, tongue, and people, including the United States, no longer the world's superpower. And as the solar eclipses targeting our nation with a great heavenly X forewarn, the coming birth pangs will do it. They must also accomplish their task in under ten years.

E. The Simultaneous Devil Comet

Remarkably, as if all the other signs proved insufficient to secure the Church's attention, during the 2024 solar eclipse, a major comet—12P/Pons-Brooks—passed overhead and became visible to the naked eyes in the darkness of the path of totality. But because of 12P/Pons-Brooks' uniquely forked tail, astronomers nicknamed it *Devil Comet*. Twice the size of Mount Everest, it appears once every 71 years. During its approach in 2023, the "Devil Comet" then suddenly brightened by a factor of

100 times due to icy portions of its ten-mile substance breaking off, reflecting even more sunlight, thus making it visible to the eye during this pass.

But considering its end-time context, with God's imminent judgment on the white-horse rider and the removal of the last restrainer of Antichrist, what could prove timelier in the darkened sky than the appearance of the bright "Devil Comet?" Like a sign of Satan, who can appear as an angel of light, this providential comet would mark the devil's stepped-up efforts to prepare the way for his satanic emissary, Antichrist, to come in the final seven years.

Profoundly enough, the date of the solar eclipse also starts the Jewish religious New Year of Nissan 1—the month of *Passover*, *Unleavened Bread*, and *First Fruits*, the three Nissan feasts of Jesus' sacrifice, burial, and resurrection. And its timing during the eclipse therefore directs our attention back to Israel and Jerusalem, as well. In the final three and a half years of this last generation, Antichrist will sit in the Jerusalem temple and claim to be God. At the end, Christ will then return during the fall Jewish feasts to destroy the Beast at the Battle of Armageddon.

And given its prophetic context during the 2024 total solar eclipse the end-time Devil Comet points to it all.

F. The Exodus 4:8 Sign

Our sixth and last sign deals with the date itself. On occasion, the numbers of a written date can apply to a Scripture reference as a providential sign. With the 2024 eclipse, we write the date as "4/8." When looking at that number in Exodus, it then happens that that reference has an astonishing application to the sign of both solar eclipses. In Exodus 4:8, the Lord said to Moses: "If they will not believe you or listen to the first sign, they may believe the latter sign."

On first impression, how incredibly appropriate that providential reference appears in relation to the signs of the two eclipses! As some point out, we saw the first eclipse in 2017, and seven years later, the second in 2024. And while they can't discern its meaning with assurance, they say the Great America

Eclipse in 2017 served as the first sign and the one in 2024 as the second. But if they can't discern the meaning of either eclipse with any certainty, how can they say these two solar signs apply to Exodus 4:8? If the Church didn't see or understand the meaning of the first one, what must it see and understand to believe in the second?

It could be, as some think, that the seven *Salem's* in the 2017 eclipse presented seven offers of peace, while seven years later the seven Nineveh's presented seven threats of judgment due to our lack of repentance. The eclipses also included the Civil War signs. Yet, what did all that mean in concrete terms? If people missed God's offer of peace in the first eclipse, would they suddenly believe in his approaching judgment upon seeing the second one? Not likely. And if people couldn't perceive God's meaning in either one, how could the Exodus 4:8 references apply to the two eclipses?

But once more, their context means everything.

In fact, the stunning significance of Exodus 4:8 lies in something far more profound than the two eclipses themselves. On 9/11, we entered the end-time generation, a truth the Church to this day doesn't recognize. It began with Jesus' *first sign*: the first birth pang and the white-horse rider, thereby fulfilling the Rev. 6:1-2 and Matt. 24:6 prophecies. But not believing in the Lord's first sign on 9/11, maybe the Church will believe in his *second sign*: namely, the second of the Four Horsemen of the Apocalypse who will fulfill Rev. 6:3-4 and Matt. 24:7 by launching a nuclear world war that leads to famine and pestilence that will kill a quarter of Earth's people.

That destruction will be hard to miss, even for a blind, deceived, disobedient, uninformed Church. As the Exodus 4:8 sign implies, once the second sign occurs, the horrible specificity and quantification of the coming Revelation prophesies will make them hard to deny. Yet, for millions of oblivious people, it will be too late by then for them. And soon after, the potential eruption of Yellowstone's supervolcano and the shattering impact of an asteroid will shake the Earth on its axis, perhaps destroying America's breadbasket, all by the late summer of 2027.

In truth, God has spoken volumes through the 2017/2024 total solar eclipses over America. Through these two sober signs, the Lord has graciously forewarned us of momentous judgments ahead. The key to understanding their meaning, however, lies chiefly in knowing their prophetic end-time context. Without knowing that, we could only speculate about what they might mean, if anything. But we do know. God's end-time program began in 2001. Nothing will change it. By the end of this generation, every nation will serve Antichrist, including the United States of America, which must be brought low for that to occur.

But for those who still hold out hope for a political deliverance that will never happen. Nuclear world war, famine, and pandemics will see to it. And for those tiresome critics and skeptics who dismiss any meaning at all in the two eclipses, the events to come should also jolt them from their unwarranted complacency and self-satisfaction. The fact that they failed to recognize the end-time generation before their eyes for two decades should rather humble them and cause them to repent of their blindness and unbelief.

The bottom line? I believe the Lord has warned: "Yet forty months and America will be overthrown."

And counting from April 8, 2024, we may have only forty weeks before the Lord begins to pour out his wrath in earnest upon us through the next four birth pangs. A new judgment could strike the United States every nine months for almost three and a half years, beginning with nuclear world war in January 2025.

Though it now seems hard to believe it could happen before then, may God grant us a last great awakening while we have time! Our only hope rests in Jesus Christ and his coming kingdom.

"The heavens declare the Glory of God; and the firmament proclaims the Work of His Hands." Psalm 19:1

Notes

Notes

Notes